THE POLES

Jamie Voss

Sally Ride
Science

Our Changing Climate
THE POLES

CONTENTS

THE ENDS OF THE EARTH

Earth is getting warmer—its air is getting warmer, its oceans are getting warmer, and its lands are getting warmer. This is affecting living things around the globe—from tadpoles to trees, and from penguins to people.

Earth's poles provide a front-row seat for climate change. The polar regions cap Earth like a pair of baseball caps. The Arctic is the northern hemisphere's "cap." The Antarctic is the southern hemisphere's cap.

The Arctic is clearly changing. It's changing faster than any other place on Earth.

The Antarctic is also changing. The warming of the ocean that surrounds it is one reason that glaciers and ice shelves on this icy continent are disintegrating.

What will climate change mean for us? Let's find out what some of the world's best climate detectives have uncovered about these frozen places and take a peek at what's happened in the past, what's happening now, and what may happen to our planet in the future.

The polar regions hold clues to our climate's past and future. These Adélie penguins in Antarctica are just one species already affected by global climate change.

The Arctic

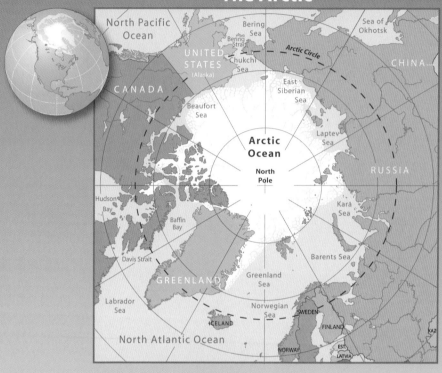

North Pacific Ocean · Bering Sea · Sea of Okhotsk · Bering Strait · Arctic Circle · UNITED STATES (Alaska) · CHINA · Chukchi Sea · CANADA · East Siberian Sea · Beaufort Sea · Laptev Sea · Arctic Ocean · North Pole · RUSSIA · Hudson Bay · Kara Sea · Baffin Bay · Davis Strait · Barents Sea · GREENLAND · Greenland Sea · Labrador Sea · Norwegian Sea · SWEDEN · ICELAND · FINLAND · KAZ · North Atlantic Ocean · NORWAY · EST. · LATVIA

Arctic, Top of the World

The Arctic is an ocean surrounded by land. In fact, the North Pole doesn't have any solid ground to plant a "pole" in. It's just an ice-covered spot in the middle of the big, icy Arctic Ocean. There is plenty of land surrounding this ocean, though, including parts of Greenland, Canada, Alaska, Russia, Finland, Sweden, and Norway.

Not So Green Greenland

Someone sure gave Greenland the wrong name. This big Arctic country in the North Atlantic Ocean is not exactly green. In fact, it's mostly covered with ice—the second-biggest ice sheet on Earth, as much as 3 kilometers (about 2 miles) thick.

The Antarctic

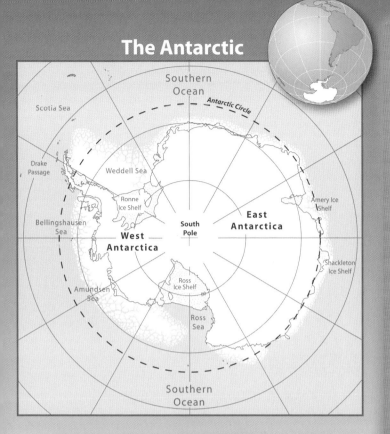

Southern Ocean

Antarctic Circle

Scotia Sea

Drake Passage

Weddell Sea

Ronne Ice Shelf

Bellingshausen Sea

West Antarctica

South Pole

East Antarctica

Amery Ice Shelf

Shackleton Ice Shelf

Ross Ice Shelf

Amundsen Sea

Ross Sea

Southern Ocean

Being There

Critters and Visitors

Who lives in Antarctica? Its permanent population is mostly penguins, seals, birds, and fish. The few humans chilling out there are mainly scientists who come for short periods to work at supercool research stations, including Byrd Station, right at the South Pole. What do they do there? On any given day, they may snowmobile or sled across the ice, deploy buoys to the bottom of the Southern Ocean, collect microbes from under the sea ice, or drill ice cores to figure out what the climate was like long ago.

Antarctica, Way Down Under

At Earth's southern pole is a supercold, windy continent called Antarctica. It's a huge slab of land completely surrounded by water—just the opposite of the Arctic. This continent is completely covered by a sheet of ice, as much as 4.3 kilometers (2.7 miles) thick. It's the largest ice sheet on our planet. Seventy percent of all the fresh water on Earth is locked up in Antarctica's ice.

West Antarctica

The skinny "thumb" of Antarctica is called West Antarctica. The ice sheet covering West Antarctica is separate from the ice sheet covering the rest of Antarctica.

Byrd Station was inside a dome until drifting snow buried it. In 2006 the station was moved into the new Amundsen-Scott South Pole Station (above, left) a few yards away.

CHANGE IN THE AIR

Is climate just a fancy word for weather? No. Climate is related to weather, but it's not the same. Weather is what you see when you look out the window. Climate in your hometown is the average weather you can expect where you live. But you can also talk about the climate of a country or a continent or the whole planet.

Heating Up

Earth is getting warmer. That means climates around the world are changing. They're not all changing at the same rate or in the same way—but they're all changing. And that's affecting everything on our planet in one way or another.

Light of Our Lives

That big yellow ball in the sky, the Sun, powers our climate. The Sun constantly emits energy in all directions. Fortunately, a small part of it falls on Earth. Sunlight provides the light and heat that we depend on to live.

Warming Our World

The sunlight that strikes our oceans and lands is absorbed at the surface and warms the planet. The warm surface then tries to cool off by radiating the heat back toward space. If this heat could make it out through the atmosphere as easily as the sunlight makes it in, our planet would be much colder than it is. But not so fast! A few gases in the atmosphere—the greenhouse gases—absorb some of the heat before it escapes into space. They trap the heat and make our planet warmer than it otherwise would be. Yes, this is the greenhouse effect (right).

Only One Percent

Not all gases are greenhouse gases. In fact, about 99 percent of our air is made of gases that are NOT— oxygen and nitrogen! But without the other one percent, there would be no greenhouse effect on our planet. You might think that would be a good thing. Think again.

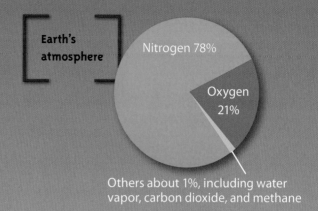

Earth's atmosphere

Nitrogen 78%

Oxygen 21%

Others about 1%, including water vapor, carbon dioxide, and methane

Hello, Greenhouse Gases

The most important greenhouse gases are water vapor, carbon dioxide, and methane. They're nothing new. They were floating in Earth's air long before there were people on the planet. And though they're only a tiny percentage of our air, those few molecules provide a greenhouse effect that warms Earth. If there were no water vapor or carbon dioxide in our air, Earth would be about 33°C (59°F) colder than it is! Our planet would be one big ice ball.

Okay, That's Enough

If the greenhouse gases in our air keep Earth from freezing, what's wrong with adding more of them? Because those gases that we're sending into the air are causing even more warming. And that's affecting our whole planet.

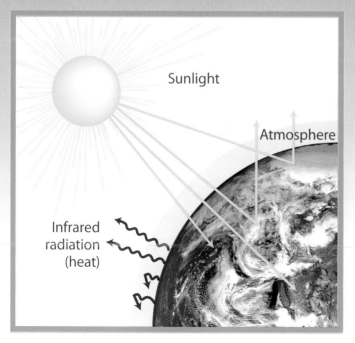

Sunlight

Atmosphere

Infrared radiation (heat)

As carbon dioxide and other greenhouse gases from car and factory fumes build up in the air, our planet is getting warmer and warmer. Uh-oh. Greenhouse overload.

Back to the Future

Climate change is nothing new. Over Earth's long history there have been cooler times, like the Ice Age 15,000 years ago. And there have been warmer times, like the tropical dinosaur days that ended 65 million years ago. In the past, these climate changes were usually triggered by natural shifts in the Earth-Sun orbit, or changes in the amount of sunlight reaching Earth. That's not the case today.

Who, Us?

This time, climate change is different. Humans are the cause. How did we do that? We've changed the atmosphere . . . much faster than it's ever been changed before. Many of the things we do—driving cars, flying in planes, lighting our cities, and making things in factories—add greenhouse gases to the air. And we're adding lots of them.

How Do They Know?

Aloha, CO_2

Before 1958, no one knew how much carbon dioxide was in the atmosphere. That year, a young scientist named Charles Keeling set up a monitoring station near the top of Mauna Loa, the largest volcano in Hawaii, to find out. He measured the amount of carbon dioxide in the air continuously for many years. His measurements are now one of the most famous graphs in science.

The Keeling Curve (right) shows that the amount of carbon dioxide in the air has gone up every year. When the measurements started, there were about 315 molecules of carbon dioxide out of every 1 million molecules of air—or parts per million (ppm). Today, there are 385 ppm of carbon dioxide! This is a huge increase in just 50 years.

315 ppm
1958

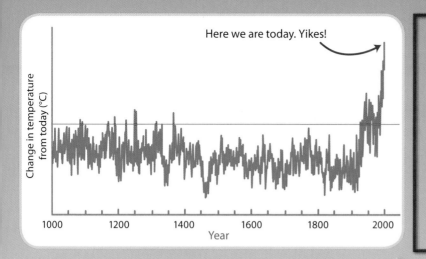

Here we are today. Yikes!

Change in temperature from today (°C)

Year
1000 1200 1400 1600 1800 2000

Compared to daily shifts in weather, climate change is subtle and hard to measure. It took scientists years to be sure it was real. But it is. In the last century, Earth's climate has warmed about 0.8°C (1.5°F). That may not sound like much, but it's the fastest our planet's global average temperature has changed in 1,000 years.

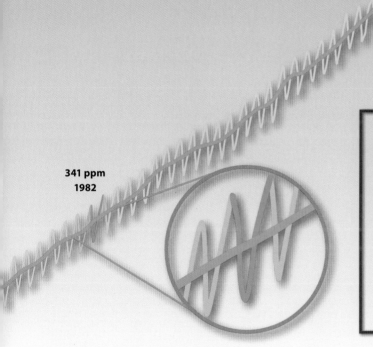

385 ppm
2008

341 ppm
1982

What causes those squiggles? Plants! The graph goes down in the spring, when plants in the northern hemisphere grow and suck in carbon dioxide as part of photosynthesis. It goes back up in the fall, when leaves drop from the trees and many plants go dormant. The squiggles show Earth "breathing." But Earth's breathing is the opposite of ours—it inhales carbon dioxide and exhales oxygen.

Warming Signs

So it's getting warmer. What's the big deal? Well, scientists have already measured many changes all around the planet. The oceans are warmer. Glaciers on mountains and ice caps are shriveling. There's more rain in the northeastern U.S., and storms are more intense. There's less rain in the parched southwestern U.S. And ecosystems everywhere are changing.

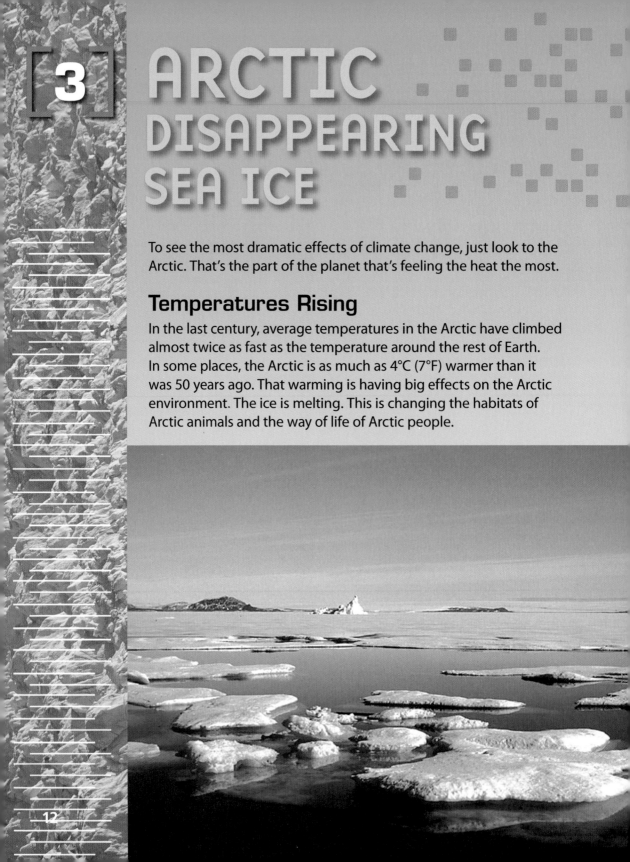

[3] ARCTIC
DISAPPEARING
SEA ICE

To see the most dramatic effects of climate change, just look to the Arctic. That's the part of the planet that's feeling the heat the most.

Temperatures Rising

In the last century, average temperatures in the Arctic have climbed almost twice as fast as the temperature around the rest of Earth. In some places, the Arctic is as much as 4°C (7°F) warmer than it was 50 years ago. That warming is having big effects on the Arctic environment. The ice is melting. This is changing the habitats of Arctic animals and the way of life of Arctic people.

What's the Big Idea?

Put Away That Parka

The warmer water in the Arctic radiates more heat into the air. That's one reason the temperature's going up faster there than anywhere else on the planet.

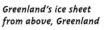

4 U 2 Do

Melt Down

Here's an icy experiment to try. Take two measuring cups, each two cups or bigger. In one, float a few ice cubes in lots of water up to the one-cup line. Tightly pack the second measuring cup full of ice cubes. Add just enough water to bring the water level to the one-cup line. Predict what will happen to the water level when all the ice in both cups has melted. Record the water levels. So what's the difference between what happens when sea ice melts compared to what happens when an ice sheet melts or crumbles into the ocean?

Ice Lingo

GLACIER
A tongue of ice that moves slowly downhill

Riggs Glacier, Glacier Bay, Alaska

ICE SHEET
Ice over land

Greenland's ice sheet from above, Greenland

ICE SHELF
Permanent ice that floats on sea but is attached to land

Ross Ice Shelf, Antarctica

ICEBERG
Mass of floating ice broken off from an ice shelf or glacier

Gerlache Strait, Antarctica

SEA ICE
Ice floating on sea

Arctic Sea Ice

13

Bright White

Snow and ice are bright! They reflect 80 to 90 percent of the Sun's light that shines on them. They bounce it right back out into space. That means it doesn't heat the planet.

> Ice reflects far more light and heat back into space than water.

Melt Mania

Ice is white. Water's dark. When sea ice melts, the water under it is exposed. The dark water absorbs sunlight instead of bouncing it right back into space the way ice does. That sunlight warms the ocean—so even more sea ice melts! This fast-forward action is called "positive feedback." More heat, more melt. More melt, more heat. You get the idea!

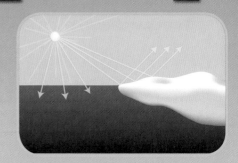

Experts Tell Us — Marika Holland

Climate Scientist
National Center for Atmospheric Research

"I sort of fell into sea-ice research," explains Marika Holland. That wasn't as hard as it sounds. Climate always intrigued her, and climate and sea ice are closely tied. Marika looks at how sea ice in the Arctic is shifting and melting. She develops computer models that predict how that affects the way Earth is changing. "It's an incredibly complicated natural system, and these are incredibly complicated models," she says. Running one model takes months!

Not long ago, Marika and her colleagues noticed something strange. "The models show these incredibly rapid decreases in annual summer ice," she said. "The Arctic goes from about like it is now to essentially ice-free in a decade." Ice cores and other information show that this speedy melting has happened before. When's the next big sea-ice melt? Marika says the models indicate it could start within 20 years.

Slice the Ice

Every year powerful ships called icebreakers smash away at the Arctic Ocean's sea ice to keep channels open for other ships—if there's ice to break! Recently, the Canadian icebreaker *Amundsen* found almost no ice to break apart as it chugged along the northern coast of Canada. Some experts estimate that summer ice at the North Pole could completely disappear as early as 2040. If you lived at the North Pole, it might be time to trade in that sled for a powerboat.

Summer Simmer

Every year there is less and less sea ice in the Arctic, especially by late summer. Some places in the Arctic have 85 fewer days of frozen ocean each year than they did just 50 years ago.

The Latest Model

Scientists "experiment" with Earth's past and future using computers. They create detailed climate models using data on the atmosphere, ice, oceans, plants, and greenhouse gases. The models re-create conditions from 1870, when we started to burn fossil fuels and to increase greenhouse gases in the atmosphere. The models are used to investigate what might happen in the future, based on different levels of greenhouse gas emissions.

Experts Tell Us

Rebecca Woodgate

Physical Oceanographer
University of Washington

For Rebecca Woodgate, becoming a physical oceanographer was a slam dunk. "I always loved the way physics tells you how everything works," says Rebecca, whose mother was also a physicist. "And I wanted to do something for the environment." Lately, Rebecca's been floating around the Bering Strait, the shallow channel that connects the Arctic Ocean to the Pacific Ocean.

Working on Coast Guard icebreakers, she measures currents, salinity (salt levels), and temperature with underwater packs of instruments called moorings. "Since about 2000, we've seen significantly more heat going north from the Pacific into the Arctic," Rebecca explains. "In three years, enough extra heat has gone through the Bering Strait to melt a region 800 kilometers (497 miles) square of one-meter-thick ice." When ice melts, it affects the ecological balance in powerful ways. For example, plankton live on the bottom of the ice. Tiny, shrimplike creatures called krill eat the plankton. Fish eat the krill. Whales eat the fish. No ice, no plankton. No plankton, no lunch!

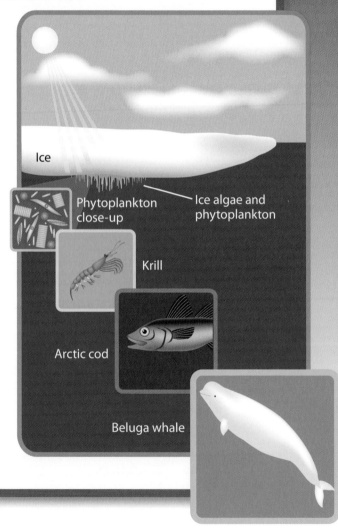

Ice

Phytoplankton close-up

Ice algae and phytoplankton

Krill

Arctic cod

Beluga whale

GRACE in Space

Greenland's ice sheet grows when it snows but shrinks when ice along the coast slips into the sea. How can scientists tell whether it's growing or shrinking? Satellites in space! The twin GRACE satellites (right) are circling Earth together. The orbits they follow are determined by Earth's gravity. The pull of gravity they feel changes ever so slightly whenever Earth's surface below—mountains, water, or ice—changes.

Whenever the satellites pass over Greenland's ice sheet, scientists can tell how the ice below them has changed. They measure the spacecrafts' orbits very precisely—any changes are reflected in the distance between the two satellites as they orbit Earth. What have scientists learned? Greenland's ice sheet is shrinking—and it's shrinking much faster now than it was even ten years ago.

What's the Big Idea?

See Level

When sea ice melts, it doesn't change sea level. Why? You guessed it. Since the ice is already in the water, it's already affecting the sea level.

Eyes on Ice

Scientists are carefully monitoring the different types of ice. What do they see? Less Arctic sea ice every year. Shriveling glaciers in Greenland. Parts of ice shelves breaking off and cracking into pieces. Drip by drop, the Arctic is melting away.

Satellites record the extent of Arctic sea ice every September. These two pictures compare September ice in 1979 (left) and 2005 (right).

Sea Ice   Greenland

Sea Ice   Greenland

4 ANTARCTICA
CRUMBLING ICE SHEETS

In Antarctica, the air has warmed a whopping 3°C (5°F) in the last 50 years. The Southern Ocean is warmer, too. Surface sea water has warmed 1°C (almost 2°F). The waters are melting Antarctica's huge floating ice shelves from underneath. The ice sheet covering West Antarctica is also shrinking. Parts of it are collapsing into the sea. When ice sheets melt or break off, they add water to the oceans. That means rising sea levels.

As Antarctic ice shelves shrink and split apart, thousands of icebergs drift into the Weddell Sea. Some icebergs are as big as 19 kilometers (12 miles) across. Heading your way.

Slip Sliding Away

Scientists watch for small blue ponds on the Antarctic ice sheets. They form from melting ice. When the water trickles down into cracks and crevices in the ice, it widens them. Scientists believe that once the meltwater that's cutting into the ice reaches the land below the ice sheet, it actually "greases" the bottom of the sheet. It makes the ice slip even faster toward the ocean. At the continent's edge, huge chunks of ice break off and crumble into the ocean. Look out below!

Splash! A waterfall of meltwater pours 30 meters (98 feet) into the Southern Ocean.

Super Slip

The rocks under the ice in West Antarctica are more slippery than rocks on other parts of the continent. That makes the West Antarctica ice sheet particularly unstable. It could slide into the sea much faster than other ice sheets. If just the West Antarctica ice sheet collapsed and melted, sea level around the world would rise 6 meters (20 feet). But don't worry yet. That's not likely to happen for many decades.

Arctic Change

Climate change is most extreme in the Arctic. These are just some of the many changes taking place.

Bering Sea

The southeast Bering Sea has warmed up a lot in recent years, with temperatures as much as 3°C (6°F) higher on the seafloor.

Penticton, British Columbia Canada

Gardeners here are happy! The annual growing season is much longer—some say 50 days longer—than it was 100 years ago.

Edmonton, Alberta Canada

Trembling aspen trees are blooming 26 days sooner in the spring than they did in 1900. Warm weather's coming earlier.

Baker Lake, Nunavut Canada

The buzz around here is . . . fewer mosquitoes! They breed in shallow ponds in the permafrost. Less permafrost makes for fewer ponds and fewer places for mosquitoes to breed.

Map labels:
- North Pacific Ocean
- Penticton
- Edmonton
- Bering Sea
- Bering Strait
- UNITED STATES
- Alaska
- Chukchi Sea
- Northern Canada
- Barrow, Alaska
- Beaufort Sea
- CANADA
- Tundra Line
- Banks Island
- Baker Lake
- Hudson Bay
- Ellesmere Island
- Igloolik, Foxe Island
- Baffin Bay
- Davis Strait
- GREENLAND
- Labrador Sea
- ICELAND
- North Atlantic Ocean

Igloolik, Foxe Island

Warmer weather has cut the Inuit people's annual hunting days in half and made the ice dangerously thin for travel.

Barrow, Alaska

No seal meat for polar bears again tonight—they couldn't reach the seals. Not enough chunks of sea ice to use as stepping stones. Looks like the menu is garbage again.

Siberia (Alaska and Northern Canada, too)

Melting permafrost—frozen soil—may release tons of the greenhouse gases methane and carbon dioxide into the atmosphere.

Banks Island, Nunavut Canada

Red-breasted robins have begun to turn up in the spring. They are so new and unexpected that the local language doesn't even have a name for this bird.

Ellesmere Island

In August 2005 the Ayles Ice Shelf broke free, becoming a huge iceberg.

Tundra Line

In the far north, it's too cold for trees to grow. The line where forests fade is called the treeline. The treeline is migrating north as conditions warm up.

Greenland

Glaciers that flow from the Greenland ice sheet into the North Atlantic Ocean are retreating every year.

Iceland

At the present rate of melt, nearly half of Iceland's glaciers could be gone by 2100.

Sea of Okhotsk

Siberia

Arctic Circle

East Siberian Sea

Laptev Sea

RUSSIA

Tundra Line

Kara Sea

Barents Sea

Greenland Sea

Norwegian Sea

FINLAND

SWEDEN

NORWAY

Chilling Events

Imagine watching the collapse of something almost twice as big as the state of Delaware. Scientists got a major case of the chills when they watched West Antarctica's huge Larsen B ice shelf collapse in 2002. The whole ice shelf, hundreds of meters (yards) thick, splintered into bits. The Larsen B ice shelf was history within a month. Scientists were astonished. They thought the Larsen B ice shelf would last at least 100 years.

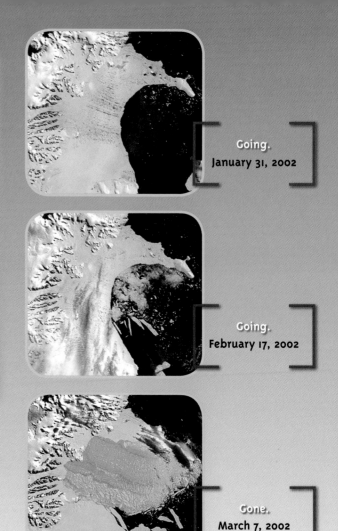

Going.
January 31, 2002

Going.
February 17, 2002

Gone.
March 7, 2002

What's the Big Idea?

Half 'n Half

Warmer water takes up more space than cooler water. So as the oceans warm up, the water expands. That makes sea level go up. Experts estimate that sea level around the world has gone up about 15 to 20 centimeters (6 to 8 inches) in the last century. About half that rise is because the water has gotten warmer and expanded. The other half is from melted ice added to the oceans.

Snorkel Cities

Inch by inch sea level is on the rise. By 2100, the sea level could rise as much as 1 meter (over 3 feet) in some places. So what? So wet! From Miami to Tokyo, from Calcutta to Buenos Aires, higher ocean levels could flood out millions of people living in low-lying places around the globe.

These maps show Florida today (left) and how much of Florida would disappear (right) if the sea level rose just one meter. The red areas would all be underwater.

4 U 2 Do

Rise Up

Melting ice can speak volumes. How much would seas rise around the world if the following had a major meltdown? Do the math. We did two to get you started.

Location	Volume (km³)	Potential Sea Level Rise (m)
East Antarctica ice sheet	26,039,200	64.6
West Antarctica ice sheet	3,262,000	6.1
Antarctica Peninsula	227,100	_____
Greenland	2,620,000	_____
All other ice caps, ice fields, and valley glaciers	180,000	_____
Total	31,544,830	78.2

Check out your answers on page 38.

POLAR PEOPLE

Four million people call the Arctic home. They are used to living in extreme cold. What will a warmer Arctic mean to them?

Around the North Pole (clockwise from upper left), Inupiat woman staying warm in her thick parka, Alaska; girl ice fishing, Iceland; climbers exploring an ice tube, Iceland; herders snowmobiling to check on their reindeer, Norway; Inuit boy playing with sled dogs, Canada.

De-iced

Inuit people are supertuned to their environment since they spend much of their time outdoors hunting and fishing. They travel and hunt on sea ice. The Inuit have noticed some real changes in the last 50 years. Caribou are skinnier. There is less snow in the winter. The ice is thinner, so travel is more treacherous.

Greener Greenland

Being a farmer in Greenland wouldn't be easy. There's that annoying glacier taking up your best field. And you've got the shortest growing season this side of an iceberg. But global warming is cheering up some Greenlanders. The glacier's shrinking and flowers are blooming where there used to be ice. Never mind the rising sea level, let's grow strawberries!

[Greenland is getting greener as permafrost and ice melt away.]

Stuck in the Muck

It may seem odd, but the Arctic trucking season is winter. That's when the soil and lakes are frozen enough to support temporary roads. In the 1970s, Alaska had over 200 days a year of winter roads. Now that's down to less than 100 days a year. Arctic truckers are getting stuck in the muck!

You Crack Me Up

Deep layers of frozen soil called permafrost can be up to 1 kilometer (0.6 miles) thick. When permafrost melts, it turns to a mushy mess. That can cause two big problems. First, roads and buildings built on permafrost collapse. Second, lots of carbon dioxide wafts into the air. Why? Tons of grasses and plant roots are frozen in the permafrost. But when the permafrost melts, bacteria attack the thawing plant pieces, releasing carbon dioxide as they digest them. This carbon dioxide adds to the greenhouse gas overload.

Oops. The permafrost under this house in Alaska melted.

On Thin Ice

Athabaskan communities in Alaska use sea ice to hunt. Now the ice is thinning dangerously. Bad news for hunters traveling across the ice on snowmobiles to reach the good fishing and hunting grounds. Good news for the fish and whales, like this beluga whale.

Mucho Methane

Yikes! Thawing permafrost also releases methane, another greenhouse gas. Sometimes when permafrost melts, pools of muddy water form. As the thawed plants in the water decay, methane bubbles out of the water and into the air. Here we go again. The extra methane accelerates the greenhouse effect even more.

Higher and Drier

Inupiat people have lived around Shishmaref, Alaska for 4,000 years. Their coastal village used to be protected by sea ice. But now the sea ice is disappearing and storms carve away at the shore. Houses are crumbling into the sea. The people of Shishmaref have to leave their island and move to a higher, safer location.

Shishmaref, Alaska is crumbling into the sea. These two pictures were taken before and after a storm. Look how much closer the barrel is to the edge of the water in the second picture.

Special Delivery?

In late October 2006, residents of Igloolik, near Baffin Island in northern Canada, were surprised to see a ship arrive. The sea there is usually frozen by then. If ships could cross the Arctic all year round, it would change shipping patterns and bring more goods to remote Arctic communities. Some predict that this could help the economy. But other northerners prefer the old days when winter isolation helped preserve Inuit culture.

Tick Tick Tick

As climate warms, habitats expand and disease can spread. In Sweden, one species of disease-carrying tick (*Ixodes ricinus*) is on the move. This bitty bug keeps turning up "fur"-ther and "fur"-ther north, on pets and other critters.

[6] TELL TAILS

Animals and plants that live in Earth's most extreme places are terrifically tough in some ways—and decidedly delicate in others. Polar life is a balance of sea ice and open water, marine life and polar animals. Climate change is changing the balance. It's changing entire ecosystems.

Some Like It Cold

Ice is nice if you're an Adélie penguin (above). These cute critters nest on floating rafts of sea ice. With less ice every year, Adélie penguins in Antarctica have taken a nose dive—in some places there are 75 percent fewer of them than there were in the 1970s. Some have popped up closer to the pole where it's colder.

Two chinstrap chicks (far left) huddle against their father. Can you guess how chinstraps got their name? A Gentoo (left) heads out for a swim. They're the fastest penguin swimmers around, clocking in at 36 kilometers (22 miles) an hour.

Some Like It Warm

Chinstrap and Gentoo penguins are birds of a different feather. They hunt in open water, preferring a home where ice doesn't roam. In the last 50 years, these penguins have moved into parts of Antarctica where summer ice is no longer in the way.

Polar Bear Plunge

Polar bears in the Beaufort Sea are in trouble. They live on sea ice, and they travel on the ice to hunt for seals that thrive in near-shore water. But lately there's less ice near the shore. That means polar bears can't reach the seals. No seals, no lunch.

This mother polar bear keeps her cubs close to keep them warm. Polar bears spend most of their lives on the sea ice.

Bye-Bye, Birdie?

On Cooper Island, near Barrow, Alaska, seabirds called black guillemots depend on the buffet provided by sea ice. The underside of the ice supports plankton, krill, and fish. Guess who dives through cracks in the ice to eat the fish? But lately the ice has drifted too far from the island for the guillemots to reach. Buffet closed.

Drawing by H. L. Todd, from No. 10443, U. S. National Museum, collected at Eastport, Me., 1872, by Prof. S. F. Baird.

THE ALASKA POLLOCK.
Pollachius chalcogrammus (Pallas). [p. 232.]

Fish Story

The Bering Sea, between Alaska and Russia, is pollock heaven. These fish do even better without ice, so populations are up as the Bering Sea warms up. If you like fish sticks, you're in luck since most of them are made from pollock. Pass the tartar sauce.

Fun with Phenology

Scientists have a name for the way animal and plant species respond to climate. It's called phenology. It's like when robins show up much farther north than they used to as their habitat shifts, or when flowers bloom earlier. Right creature, new place. Or right place, new time.

How Do They Know?

Tag! You're It

In spring, polar bear researchers use helicopters to find bears, and then put ear tags and satellite tracking collars on them. The collars are specially programmed to fall off after a year.

Fresh polar bear tracks on sea ice in Greenland

treeline ———

Can Trees Walk?

No, but they can grow farther north as the Arctic warms up. Same with everything else, from bushes to birds. One study reported that as Earth warms, habitats are shifting an average of about 6 kilometers (about 4 miles) farther north every decade. Better pack up the birdhouse and call the moving van.

Experts Tell Us

Scott Schliebe

Polar Bear Project Leader
U.S. Fish and Wildlife Service

How do you sample a polar bear before he samples you? "From a vehicle, if possible," explains polar bear researcher Scott Schliebe. "Sampling" just means watching. Scott has had his eye on Alaska's polar bears for more than 20 years.

Bears prefer chilling out on near-shore sea ice, where they can hunt for seals, he says. But his research shows that every year the sea ice is moving farther from shore and breaking up earlier in the spring. Bad news for bears. They need seals to put on pounds to survive winter. "We're seeing more bears on land. These bears are basically fasting," explains Scott. The hungry bears scavenge whatever food they can, like whale carcasses left over from Inuit hunting. "The future for polar bears is quite grim," Scott says.

[7] DEEP SECRETS

Wouldn't it be cool if we could look back in time and learn what happened in the past? For Earth's climate we can. The answers are frozen in polar ice, as if Earth were keeping a diary.

Where Sledding Never Ends

In Antarctica and Greenland, summer is so cold that snow doesn't even melt. It just builds up year after year. Eventually, all those layers of snow (below) add up to thick ice sheets. The oldest layers are on the bottom. The newest layers are on the top.

Paleo-what?

Paleoclimatologists study ancient climates. They have clever ways to decode what the climate was like thousands of years ago by analyzing those old layers of ice.

Stripes of Time

To get their data, paleoclimatologists drill deep into ancient ice. Then they pull out long cores of the ice. The cores have faint stripes. Each stripe is one year's worth of snow. Scientists know how long ago a layer of ice was made just by counting the layers! Paleoclimatologists reconstruct ancient temperatures by analyzing oxygen in the ancient layers.

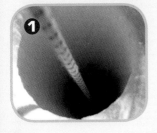

❶ Drilling down. Down.
❷ Shaking the core.
❸ Success! Ancient ice.

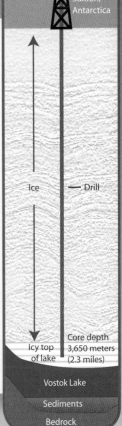

Vostock Drilling Station, Antarctica

Ice — Drill

Icy top of lake

Core depth 3,650 meters (2.3 miles)

Vostok Lake

Sediments

Bedrock

How Do They Know?

Counting the Years

In Greenland, one year's worth of old compacted snow can be 0.5 meters (1.5 feet) thick. In very dry Antarctica, annual layers are too thin to be visible without a microscope. Paleoclimatologists use different methods to count how many years an ice core represents. For example, summer snow is different from winter snow—it's coarser. So a layer of coarser ice crystals indicates one summer's snowfall.

And That's in *Summer*

Drilling ice in Greenland is no picnic. First, there's the cold—minus 20°C (minus 4°F) on a good day. To keep warm, you need goose-down coats and shoes so thick they're nicknamed "Frankenstein boots." Then there's the sticky drilling fluid that everyone gets covered with. It's a great time, say the scientists!

Fossil Air

As one layer of snow falls on another, small pockets of air get trapped in the snow. As the snow gets packed into ice, the air pockets become tiny bubbles in the ice. The older the layer, the older the air trapped inside. It's fossil air!

CSI: Antarctica

An air bubble contains gases from the atmosphere—like nitrogen, oxygen, and carbon dioxide—at the time the air was trapped. Climate detectives can analyze this ancient air to learn how much carbon dioxide was in the atmosphere when the bubble formed. Better than fingerprints!

What's the Big Idea?

The Core of the Matter

Analyzing ice cores has told us a lot about our changing climate. This graph shows two big discoveries.

- Look at the zigzag lines—Earth's temperature and the amount of carbon dioxide in the air go up and down, hand in hand.
- Carbon dioxide in the air is higher now than it's been in at least 650,000 years. (Yes, 650,000 years!)

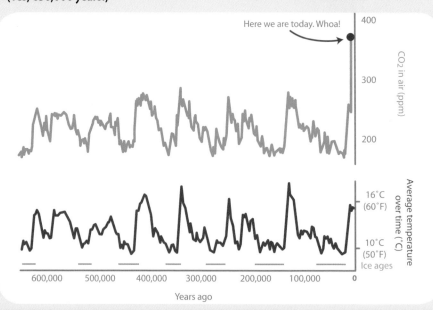

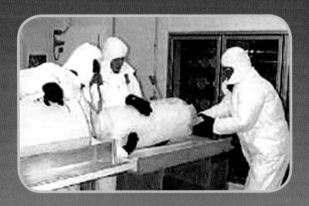

Big Freezer. It's a nice summer day in Denver. Why are those scientists wearing down coats? They're in the big freezers at the National Ice Core Laboratory, where ice cores from all over the Arctic and Antarctic are kept for study.

Keep Drilling

The ice sheet covering Antarctica averages over 2.4 kilometers (1.5 miles) thick. That's *millions* of years of snow. One drilling core in East Antarctica burrowed over 3 kilometers (1.9 miles) into the ice. The layers of ice on the bottom of the core were more than one million years old. Greenland's ice sheet is no slouch, either. One ice core in Greenland took four years to drill. It went more than 3 kilometers (1.9 miles) deep—but only 200,000 years back in time because a season's worth of snowfall is so thick.

Experts Tell Us James White

Paleoclimatologist
University of Colorado

Twenty years ago, paleoclimatologist Jim White was part of a team studying ice. They decided to focus on just a few years of ice at a time. What they found stunned them. Big climate shifts—which they thought had taken thousands of years—had actually happened much, much faster. "I realized these dramatic changes were happening within 50 years—the span of a human lifetime," Jim says. "For me, that took paleoclimatology from being just something intriguing to being something of great public interest."

Nearly every summer, Jim travels to Greenland to study more ice cores. He's searching for early warning signals of abrupt climate change. "If abrupt climate change has a threshold, we need to find it because we might be approaching it," he says.

FULL CIRCLE

Even though the poles may be thousands of miles away, we affect them and they affect us. We're all part of Earth's delicate natural balance.

We've already changed the climate of the polar regions dramatically. Like a cool whisper, the changes at the poles are warning us about our warming future. Is there anything we can do?

One World

Climate change is a global challenge. Every country in the world needs to do its part—to reduce its use of fossil fuels and emissions of greenhouse gases. People from all over the world are coming up with creative ways to do this, from using renewable energy sources to using less polluting cars, trains, and ships, to developing "greener" methods of agriculture. Can we do it? Yes we can!

U 2

You can help take the steam out of climate change, too. Encourage your family to drive less and carpool more. That means less carbon dioxide released into the air. Use energy-efficient light bulbs. Use recycled or secondhand products. Recycle paper, bottles, plastics, and cans—reduce the amount of stuff going into landfills. You'll ease the drain on Earth's resources, reduce reliance on fossil fuels, and help keep greenhouse gases out of the air.

The world will thank you later. Arctic people, penguins, and polar bears will thank you now.

atmosphere (n.) A layer of gases surrounding a planet or moon, held in place by the force of gravity. (p. 8, 10, 15, 21, 34)

climate (n.) Prevailing weather conditions for an ecosystem, including temperature, humidity, wind speed, cloud cover, and rainfall. (p. 5, 7, 14, 30)

ecosystem (n.) All of the living organisms, plant, animal, and microscopic species, in a given area that interact with each other and their surrounding environment. (p. 11, 28)

food chain (n.) A series of living organisms related to each other as prey and predator. (p. 16, 29)

fossil fuel (n.) Nonrenewable energy resources such as coal, oil, and natural gas that are formed from the compression of plant and animal remains over hundreds of millions of years. (p. 15, 36, 37)

greenhouse effect (n.) The warming that occurs when certain gases (greenhouse gases) are present in a planet's atmosphere. Visible light from the Sun penetrates the atmosphere of a planet and heats the ground. The warmed ground then radiates infrared radiation back toward space. If greenhouse gases are present, they absorb some of that radiation, trapping it and making the planet warmer than it otherwise would be. (p. 8, 9, 26)

greenhouse gases (n.) Gases such as carbon dioxide, water vapor, and methane that absorb infrared radiation. When these gases are present in a planet's atmosphere, they absorb some of the heat trying to escape the planet instead of letting it pass through the atmosphere, resulting in a greenhouse effect. (p. 8, 9, 10, 21, 26, 36)

habitat (n.) A place where individual organisms of a particular species live. It provides the types of food, shelter, temperature, and other conditions needed for survival. (p. 12, 27, 30, 31)

photosynthesis (n.) Process by which plants use energy from sunlight to convert carbon dioxide and water into food (in the form of sugar). Oxygen is released in the process. (p. 11)

phytoplankton (n.) Aquatic, free-floating, microscopic, photosynthetic organisms. (p. 16)

Answers

4 U 2 Do, page 23
Antarctica— 0.56
Greenland— 6.49 (or 6.5 rounded up)
All other— .446 (or .45 rounded up)

IMAGE CREDITS

© Image Plan/Corbis: Cover. NASA: bookplate background, p.13 middle. p. 17 bottom. NOAA: bookplate top left, center and bottom, p. 30 top. EPA: bookplate top right. Iowa State University Extension: bookplate top right lower. FWS: bookplate left center, p. 20 middle, p. 25 bottom. Caroline S. Rogers/USGS: bookplate left center lower, p. 20 middle. Keith Robinson: Bookmark. Melissa Rider, National Science Foundation: pp. 4-5. Ragnar Th. Sigurdsson: p. 6, p. 24 center. Commander John Bortniak, NOAA Corps: p. 7 inset, p. 13 top. Scot Jackson NSF: p. 7. Tim Fitzharris: p. 8. Michael Hambrey: p. 12, p. 25 top, p. 29 bottom. Monterey Bay Aquarium Research Institute: p. 13 middle. Rear Admiral Harley D. Nygren, NOAA Corps (ret.): p. 13 middle. © C. A. Linder, WHOI: p. 13 bottom. Genny Anderson: p. 14 top. National Center for Atmospheric Research: p. 14 bottom. ArcticNet: p. 15. NASA Earth System Science Pathfinder Program: p. 17 top. Pete Bucktrout, British Antarctic Survey: p. 18. Mike Vecchione, NOAA: p. 19 top. Pedro Skvarca: p. 19 bottom. T. Laycock: p. 20 top. Bigfoto.com: p. 20 bottom. Bryan & Cherry Alexander Photography: p. 21 top, p. 24 top, p. 30 bottom. Luciano Napolitano: p. 21 bottom. NSIDC/Ted Scambos: p. 22. Weiss and Overpeck, The University of Arizona: p. 23 top. W. Hagen, University of Kiel/Institute of Polar Ecology: p. 23 bottom. Aaron Collins/FWS: p. 24 bottom. UCLA: p. 26 top. U.S. Navy: p. 26 middle. Ólafur Ingólfsson www.hi.is/~oi/index.htm: p. 26 bottom. Nome Nugget Newspaper: p. 27 top. JC Schou/Biopix: p. 27 bottom. Patrick Rowe NSF: p. 28, p. 29 bottom. Lieutenant Philip Hall, NOAA: p. 29 top, p. 37 top. Steve Armstrup/FWS: p. 29 middle. Wil Meinderts/Foto Natura: p. 31 top. Dan Frerich NSF: p. 32. Reto Stöckli, NASA's Earth Observatory: p. 33. NICL: p. 35 top. Earth-saver.com: p. 36 top right. Seth Loader: p. 36 middle right. Daimler Chrysler: p. 36 bottom. EPA: p. 36 bottom left.